# But Still, Music

ISBN 978-1-7370520-3-6

Library of Congress Control Number 2022937764

Cover and book design by Lauren Grosskopf

*Pleasure Boat Studio books are available through:*

Baker & Taylor, Ingram Distribution Worldwide,

Amazon.com, barnesandnoble.com

&

Pleasure Boat Studio: A Nonprofit Literary Press

www.pleasureboatstudio.com

Seattle, Washington

# But Still, Music

ANNE PITKIN

Pleasure Boat Studio: A Nonprofit Literary Press

To the Memory of
Elizabeth Pitkin Danu
1961-2018

# CONTENTS

## I.

# II.

# I

*I am carried in my shadow*
*like a violin*
*in its black case*

—Thomas Tranströmer

# MOCKINGBIRD

I heard the mockingbird:
robin, cardinal, blue jay, car horn,
one bird arguing in many voices.

I thought I'd escaped the secrets,
the lies behind which the smiling grownups hid—
whispers that hurt the child, telling me

I was not pretty.

\*

I heard the mockingbird
the day my mother died, and I was free
of the last attachment.

That day, the sun clamored
into the windows of the mausoleum
our old home had become.

A cardinal streaked from the maple,
an ember over the dry yard.
It landed on the rusted pole

for the long vanished martin house
and flew away.

\*

I heard the mockingbird
in the elm partway down the bluff,
where Michael and I found—we were certain—
the shell of a crashed plane.


\*


Someone asked me after Mother's funeral,
*Are you Episcopalian or Presbyterian?*

*Yes.* I answered. *Guilty.*

# THE FIRST HOME

*—for Michael, wherever you are,*
*best friend of my childhood*

You sat by the street, howling
so loud we heard you and brought you in.
Your mother had sent you to bed again without dinner.

You'd been late. Didn't hear her calling,
the two of us not noticing how late.

The mothers are dead.
The fathers are dead.

Jays scold, beautiful
and harsh. They know everything.
Can you hear them?

We lived on the same bluff
across the street from each other.
We quarreled, hitched rides on old Fines's garbage wagon,
played all day from house to house.

Where are you?
The jays know. Scolding all day long.
But where are you?

Once, years ago, we spoke by phone.
*I'll love you forever*, you wailed,
so drunk I could barely understand.

How many years
since the muddy Red River unrolled from under our bluff
along the future's unreadable maps?

I have a photo, the two of us holding hands
across the sprinkler, summer's first ritual.
We face the camera, laughing,
our eyes tight closed against sun and pelting water.

The maple we climbed and hid in for hours
still bends over the street. You warned me
about the Bell Witch, the perils
of Miss Sadie's fifth grade.

Once the bad boys treed us.
*Dare you to come down, sissy*, they said.

I think of trying to find you. Jays scold, *Too Late!*

One summer, after you'd been two months out of town,
your mother's old Ford pulled into the driveway.
All day I'd been waiting, all day under the maple.

You leapt out, tore across the street—

you picked me up and paused, the two of us dazed

with happiness, then spun me under the riotous sun.

# GHOST STORIES

The grownups murmured
behind lighted windows.
Michael told ghost stories
inside the willow fronds,
a flashlight's green eye
keeping us safe.

The nine o'clock train
shrieked through town.
Cicadas sawed gritty fiddles.
A hundred silent creatures
blinked in the trees
every night until the night

Michael bolted.
*They're coming, they're coming!*
he shouted. The world spun,
whistling, through the universe,
the two of us racing,
separate, blind

until Michael screamed—
I was sure they'd got him—
kept screaming, stumbled back
from the brick garden wall
his purple nose broken, face
a mess of blood and tears.

I've heard a *thunk* as a bird
flew into a window, as if the sky
had betrayed it.
Stunned, it recovered
or didn't. Afternoons go on
overturning buckets
of bronze and gold,
down the horizon that beckons
or clangs shut.

# GHAZAL FOR A PRODIGY

Michael was most himself when he danced.
An unlearned grace possessed him when he danced.

A child, he brought onto the stage
a landing heron, a deer mid-leap when he danced.

All summer, acrobatic purple martins woke the air.
He could glide like them and spiral when he danced,

adored the air he slipped through like their scalpel wings.
The air adored him when he danced,

trees bent like aunts and uncles, birds
brought news of another country when he danced.

Sissy! The town called him. Pretty girl.
He was not normal when he danced.

He gave it up. Normal meant more
to the child than joy when he danced.

It's the past, Anne. Let it go—
how grace could save him only when he danced.

# MICHAEL

He should have had a wind to sleep in.
He should have had a wren in his window,
a symphony to play for him alone,
and when, barely grown, he left,

the town should have waved and shouted
and wished him well.

# MOCKINGBIRD

I heard the mockingbird
the afternoon my mother died,
hidden in a Magnolia marking dead center
of the First Union Bank Square.

Across the street, the Cumberland shone,
its golden haze drifting inland.
The other birds had gone silent.
I looked for him. Never found him.

# OCTOBER

They ghost through the haze over the lake,

six crew boats, the only motion

this afternoon, so alive in its last moments,

I can only think Hail and Farewell,

shadow and shine, the electric season

of last lights, the recent death

of someone I remember for the first time

in years, flaring everywhere

like the pooled yellow leaves before

they disappear into the ground.

# SOUTHERN GOTHIC

Not the mourning dove, green song from across the river,
not the smell of mown grass, lunches
of wild onions, walnuts and nectar from the honeysuckle

but the scream of peacocks outside Phila's guest house
        and restaurant,
penned Great Danes bellowing and hurling themselves
against the chain link, Phila trilling

*Now y'all just go into this private room where you can*
*whoop and holler all you want to.*

Not the grandparents
teasing the children who won't eat their salad.

Mother whimpers, unable to speak, helped into her seat
by Father, who thinks this is good for her.

Father cajoles Mother, *Just try a bite, one bite*
*of this good food.* Pouting, she picks at it
with her usable left hand. Suddenly she stops, turns blue.
She's choking on the fried chicken.

Father the doctor takes her pulse, asks her what's wrong.
I jump behind her, perform the Heimlich Maneuver.
She vomits all over the table, saved.

Phila appears, rolls up the tablecloth, and snatches it off the table.
*Now, I'll just get the dessert for y'all,*
she chirps, as the children flee to the next room.
Fudge pie with whipped cream.

Mother is helped to a chaise with a wet cloth on her forehead.
We are to pretend all is well.

Back home, I help her upstairs.
At the landing, she collapses. I make a chair of my knees
and go down under her. She weighs so little.

I half carry her the rest of the way to her hospital bed.
Father says, *We've had lots of good times.*
*We'll have 'em again.*

# APRIL

She hasn't spoken since the stroke three years ago,
can't move her right arm stiffened in its sling.

The rain has stopped, so green and careless.
The dogwood shivers with sun and one robin singing.

We face each other in two lawn chairs
under the tree where rain still taps leaf to leaf.

I'm reading letters I wrote home from school
so many years ago. I must have made a face

because when I look up, she's laughing at me
as if I were still her known and funny child.

# CEDAR WAXWINGS

Mother's favorite birds,
elegant colors muted except for the yellow on the tail,
the bandit's mask, scarlet drops on each wing.

They flocked to the hackberry tree
once a year, splattering purple berries all over
the gray Plymouth parked underneath.

The waxwings were an event,
a torrent of grace, tourists passing through
our back yard into the next berry tree,
the next grove, the next state.

My mother, who tried to throttle her one life
into a shape she could live with,
loved them, their spots of red

signaling catastrophe or passion
pulsing behind the ordered world—waxwings
descending from the heavens.

They disappeared in the next hour, leaving their droppings
(she called them "calling cards") for her to clean up.

# SOUTHERN

When I ask my best friend why her mother's
maid has to work on Sunday, fixing Sunday dinner,
she tells me patiently that Sunday is a day of rest.

They call it innocence. What I had

listening out my bedroom window summer nights
to the shouting and blues beats from the taverns,
or was it the Revival in the stadium?

Mourning doves at dawn, smell of honeysuckle.

What I had—

walking barefoot on the big yard, stung by a bee
on clover, Elsie the maid to soothe me with a poultice
of baking soda and vinegar.

I didn't need money, didn't need food,
didn't need soap, running water, heat. I had Elsie

who sometimes took me with her on the bus
but wouldn't sit with me. She ate in the kitchen
with the yard man. Every night, she walked home.

It mattered—what I wore to school,
whether I played flute or oboe in the band. I had
these decisions to make.

I wore taffeta, my hair curled in Mattie Johnson's
beauty salon for the Big Dance.

Moonlight in the yard, maple shadows swarming through it.

Across the fence, where every day I heard children,
dogs barking, chickens squawking, a red house
rested on stilts.

Every year, Mother took a Christmas basket.
The boys who lived there crossed our yard to get home.
Father couldn't stop them.
I had the future. The flat world was my oyster.

# FESTIVAL

Crickets and katydids shrilled
through the summer nights,

and lightning bugs like struck match embers
floated on a sea of night air.

On-off on-off through the mist that rose evenings,
they bobbed low to the grass and slow

enough for us to catch them in our hands,
our blood illuminated, fingers red.

We were certain they lit the earth for our pleasure,
as if their amorous signaling had anything to do with us.
We trapped them in jars—all that starlight—

Later, we'd release them,
a fountain, into the dark, a cheer
then silence.

# MISS BIRDY'S BIBLE CLASS

The Jewish kids had to leave the room
when blue-haired Miss Birdy was due
with her briefcase full of Bible stories.

The rest of us, Christians, who attended
the First Presbyterian, the First Baptist, the Church of Christ
and many other churches, had to stay and listen for an hour.

The Bible, she said, was inspired by the Word.
If you needed an answer to a question,
any question, all you had to do was open the Bible,
plop your finger on the page, and there was your answer.

What should I name the kittens? *Begat.*
Who would I marry when I grew up?

Adam and Eve were run out of the garden
for eating an apple. Was it the only good one?

Abraham came THIS close to running a sword
through his own child because God told him to,
changing His mind at the last minute.

God, the same one, sent His only son
to be born on a pile of straw,
protected by the warmth of cattle hovering.
But he died young on the cross to save us sinners.

It was never too early to be a sinner.
Miss Birdy told the whole class how Andy Russell cried
when he told her he went fishing on Sunday with his daddy,
a doctor, who sometimes worked on Sunday,
*Makin' money,* Miss Birdy sniffed.

Gilmer Marable, one of the bad boys, died
of polio one summer. I wondered if he'd go to heaven.
He would, she said, if he'd been baptized.

God watches us all the time, she said.
His eye is on the sparrow. I figured He hovered
outside, like Santa Claus, peering into the window
to see if I was being good.

Summers, God retreated into the background
without Miss Birdy. Mother and I
sat together outside, looking at the stars,
the night buzzing and ringing with cicadas and crickets.

Mother told me stories of the naughty gods—
jealous Juno, philandering Jupiter, Cassiopeia
doomed to hang forever upside down in her chair
for her vanity, Cupid, dedicated to love but prone
to error and mischief. The Big Dipper—
my favorite because I could easily find it—
poured stars across the sky.

*I stretched out the heavens with my hands*
*And I ordained all their host.*

We could smell honeysuckle
when the maples sighed, leaves rustling in the still air.

# THE ROOT CHILDREN

All day they called to me from across the fence
*Whoo whoo.* I knew them from the book
*The Root Children* across whose pages they bobbed
in their flowery dresses and hats when spring called them out
of their earthen home.

I could see their house from the window
of my bedroom papered with dogwood blossoms—
the mule tied to a post, dogs howling for hours.

One afternoon, I sneaked out, down the path
by the yard to play with the root children,
onto the packed dirt, where the red house stood on stilts.
Like a real playhouse. The mother stood in the door,
"colored," barefoot.

The root children took me by the hand
and welcomed me out to where the dolls were,
gave me a corncob doll to keep.
The maid found me and yanked me home crying.

Nights late, after the root children had gone to bed,
the train wailed through town.

Tree shadows billowed on the grass,
and the air hummed with motors running the earth.

One night, a barn right by the fence
caught fire, heating the windows of my room.
I watched the giant blaze, stick figures racing
back and forth, the mule braying. Mother and Father
feared it would spark through the fence.

Then winter. Silence again. Trees bone bare.

# EVERY SUNDAY WE SING THE DOXOLOGY

*Praise God from Whom all blessings flow.*
*Praise Him all creatures here below.*
*Praise Him above, ye heavenly hosts.*
*Praise Father, Son, and Holy Ghost.*


Mr. Fenelly preaches that God loves us all—
the thief, the harlot, the money lender,
The "Coloreds," how He loved Wanda Ditmore's mother
until she sinned with the pastor of the First Baptist Church.

Old Aschel burps and mutters throughout the service.
Some say Aschel means "wild ass." But Aschel is no ass, just deaf.
*Where the hell's Billie Green*, he stage whispers during
         the silent prayer.
I look at Johnny C. He looks at Albert. This is what we came for.

Mr. Fenelly preaches about the pure in heart, about heaven,
         what's up there
and how to avoid stumbling into potholes on the Road of Life.
How God and His angels will lift us right over if we have faith

like Sarah Elizabeth McKensie, who had faith
and put her cancer into His loving arms, whose faith
abided in Him alone, and He lifted her right up into the next world.

And what of God's other creatures here below?
Please, Sir, have mercy on Mary's dying skunk, her alligator
(Albert or Alberta) hissing in the bathtub. Lord have mercy
on the Boston Bull Ursula, in a fit of pique,
hurled off the roof of the Royal York Hotel.
Where, oh where, do their sweet spirits go?

Aschel burps. I look at Johnny C. and snort.
Father tightens his grip on my knee.
I don't care about heaven without Aschel, without dogs and skunks
and grape vines, without honeysuckle and the Dairy Queen.

Praise the father torturing my knee.
Praise the Son, the brother I don't have.
Praise the Holy Ghost I run from in the summer nights
until Aschel burps his last, and I grow up.

## NASHVILLE, SUMMER RAIN
## ALL THOSE YEARS AGO

It beat on the concrete porch where, in only a diaper,
Beth hopped and squealed,
wispy hair soaked, water beading
and flinging off her back and belly.
You should have heard her—in that hard youth
we were living—shouting her tuneless ode
to the deluge, to the stunted maple in the yard,
the wallpaper in the front room beginning to peel,
the Canadian upstairs finishing his doctorate.
Her diaper slipped lower and lower
until she jumped out of it, and now,
many years later, I'm remembering that moment,
little happiness yelling through the heavy air.

# LYLE THE CROCODILE

is a three-foot-long wooden crocodile
Alan made years ago in art school—
a masterpiece—one piece of wood
carved into jointed sections.
He looks like a friendly cartoon dragon
with periscope eyes and raised nostrils.
Beth kept him in her living room for the rest of her life.
One Easter, I went to their place for brunch.
They had an egg dangling from the ceiling—
the egg of Damocles. Alan took me for a slow ride
on his motorcycle, through the neighborhood,
past the flowering plums, their loosed petals
whirling through the air, *the snows of yesteryear*.
Colette, their cat, played the piano
carefully with her right front paw, one note at a time.
They gave her to me when they moved.
She was not happy at my house
with the other cats and hid in the cupboard
with the rice and the macaroni.
I feel sad about that. I feel sad about
so many things I can't go back and fix.
I said to Beth before she died
how sorry I was to have been the mother I was
rather than the one she needed.
From time to time, I trip over Lyle,
who occupies a prominent place

near the brass cricket Beth gave me
to put on the hearth for good luck.

## THE MUSIC MAN

Seventeen, my late firstborn is singing

"Goodnight My Someone,"

Marion the Librarian's song

as she sang it in her senior musical.

She's singing

*Our star is shining*

in the mall, between

B. Dalton Books and the Bean Pod,

*Sweet dreams to carry you close to me*

a preview, drawing a crowd, drawing

a circle of yellow light around her. There she is safe,

the future unlit, harmless.

*Goodnight*

*Goodnight*

# ONE YEAR AFTER YOUR DEATH

We had an early spring last year.
I looked for you every time a breeze disturbed
the dogwood on the verge of opening.

Today is cold and blustery.
A new plague has consumed the world.
If you were alive, our phone lines would buzz all day

and I would worry about your health.
It would have been such a pleasure.

The cherry trees are bursting
like blown dandelions. Daffodils crowd their beds.

I no longer look for you. For some time now,
I've been able to see your picture without crying.

I don't like this. You are drifting farther
and farther into the past
where you do not belong.

# EMILY'S TOMATOES

She watered, researched, fed, replanted,
worried, hovered—she has harried into life
ten pots of enormous plants bent by burgeoning fruit:
big ones swelling red, big green ones,
little green ones the size of grapes,
a different fruit for each pot.
Nothing makes her happier,
she says, than tending them.
After work, she likes to water them,
sit with them sparkling in the sun.

Midwife to the entire cycle,
she started with seeds in a sunny window.
Now this tomato farm in the driveway.
How are Emily's tomatoes, the neighbors ask.

She never dreamed she could create such bounty,
never dreamed the plants would push past
bugs, mites, the weight of dirt, to escape
their husks and climb, mere strings
toward light and air,
would conquer yet new dangers—
mold, slugs, a spelunking cat.
Lady Bountiful, Tomato Queen,
she has gone forth and multiplied.
She has replenished the earth.

# REPRIEVE

The gnats are back, orbiting who knows what in front of me.

Where have you been,
my darlings, blowing in from your separate lives?

I believe I hear the Blue Bird of Happiness, its teensy beak
chipping the paint off my windowsill.

Don't pull the laundry yet! The angelic sheets are lolloping
in the sun and wind. Oh stay

for a minute, whatever you are.

## PURPLE

The snow that began with her illness

broke a quarter off the tree I planted long ago.
Purple lilacs. Her favorite color. Purple clothes, amethyst jewelry,
a purple streak in her hair.

The snow that began with her illness
stopped traffic, downed power lines.

Icicles hung from the gutter like long teeth.
The streets went silent except for the voices of children
calling, angelic, momentary.

After the snow melted, she died. Leaving us—brother,
sister, and me, her mother, unbelieving, an animal
staggering on three legs.

Spring. The remaining lilacs bloomed. The dogwood bloomed.
I wanted to imagine her in the March wind

blowing around the corner in her purple cape,

leaving this life with a faint ringing of bells,
her coloratura vaulting on the other side I don't believe in.

The snow that began with her illness melted one day
and spring came without her. How could that be?

I once saw a woman's lavender sari swirling
around her as she stepped into a whitewashed street
in Cape Town, Malay District.

An apparition brief as a scent of lilac, brief as a life, and I
will never forget her.

Spring came without my daughter. The lilac swelled to life.

It was an eviction.

Sometimes I dream I hear her crying
            *Wait, I forgot something!*

# IRIS

Behind them, the budding oaks
rise from halfway down the bluff.

Sunlight used to swell there
or rain thrown down with thunder.

A perfect child, three or so, sunny hair,
a blue dress, casts her shadow, taking a dainty step

before the long one of her grandfather,
home from work, in brown pants and tie,

a little disheveled, who proudly shelters her,
as if he could, beside the iris in full bloom,

a river of them, sky blue and nodding
at the yard's edge. A cardinal surely flashes

somewhere near. I can hear the metallic pop
as a squirrel drops a walnut on the Plymouth

parked outside the frame. How long before
someone mows the flowers down,

scraping the bulbs, and cuts the trees
to open up the view gone from from farmland to suburbs?

My child's blue dress, my long dead father's shirt
have faded as the past fades into dangerous perfection.

# THE OLD NEIGHBORHOOD

A young woman walked every day, walked and walked—
like someone desperate. That's how I see her now
in her red jacket, same shade as the thin red streak
scoring the horizon just before dark.

Along the edge of the neighborhood
my child skipped home at dusk, stopping every few minutes
to upend herself into a headstand. The city lights were blinking on
far below, profuse as spilled salt.

The air turned smoky blue those evenings,
    color of a scarf I wanted, color
of smoke fading out as it rose over the city, harmless.

One night, under a full moon, two small boys, one mine,
loped back and forth between houses, laughing at the protean
forms of their shadows.

The cat slept belly up in the middle of the street.

## DEATHBED DRAWING OF KEATS
## BY JOSEPH SEVERN

The large shadow sets off the pallor of his face,
his death the dark companion on his pillow.
Can he have been this beautiful?
Curls clinging to his forehead, the sensuous mouth, straight nose
under his high brow, lashes against his cheek?

I won't forget her perfection in these moments, skin sculpted tight
over her bones, hair damp around her face. I'm gazing at her
as she dozes, almost transparent. Opens her eyes,
*Are you ok, my mama,* she asks. I lie, *I'm ok, my daughter.*
Minutes ago, she was keening for the children she must leave.

When she was a child, walking to school,
she tried to turn around, wanting to come back. I'd wave her on.
How can I have done that? You wouldn't know,
from Severn's portrait of a young man at peace,
about his travail, torn like a limb from all he loved,

      stolen from those who loved him.

# ORIGINS

I escaped the town,
the churches, the sins, the gardens, the snakes.

Not the smell of the grave. Damp earth where the roots
are buried and course like rivers into the marrow.

The river, golden in the late sun, golden in the air,
in the street—

crickets and cicadas sawing and singing all night
outside my bedroom window.

The mockingbird called and called.

The grownups didn't hear it, listeners for weakness,
alert for the small missteps, the fruity soft spots of the spirit.

*You have to be careful! You'd be so pretty if you'd just. . .*

When my father died,
I found in his pocket the clipping:
>How to Help Your Stroke Sufferer—

my mother, unable to talk, her left arm in a sling,
the violin she practiced every morning mute in its case.

The rusted pole of the martin house still stands
at the edge of the yard, where he planted it years ago

just past the elm where the tarnished moon
tangled—do I still live there like a torn kite
in its branches, an unraveled scarf of smoke?

The day my mother died, the sun clambered into the windows.
The robins came back, as I'd last heard them,
after rain, under the dogwood.

The train still shrieks from Guthrie to Nashville.

In the stadium, where the penitent flock to the Revival,
the evangelist cries, *Mercy O' Lord!*

It's a long story. Isn't it always a long story?
The Avalon groans its dense riverboat chord all the way to Memphis
churning the river's slow, muddy currents rolling into the Mississippi.

# II

*When I was small, I heard a strange music behind the universe.*

—Hjaldor Laxness

# ORFEO

I dreamed I heard a panpipe's unappeasable music.
The teacher said "Orfeo," one song in the opera

Wounded Soldier. Aren't all soldiers wounded?
Orpheus surely played that panpipe music

for my own fallen warrior, grown, whose song
I'll never hear again, singing to her children.

*Some days,* she once said, the first time
she was sick, *I just have to sing a little.*

The sky swirled over and around,
a few stars like motes floating through.

I woke up slowly, dreaming I was tangled in sheets
that coiled and bound.

(Did she struggle to get free,
held back by a body that was done with her?)

I untangled myself endlessly and woke up
to write it down, to write down, as if I could

where I'd been, where she might be
lost or unlost. Might not want us any more.

Did I think to map the infinite? I would have
dragged her, even unwilling, back into my life.

# READING WILLIAM HEINESEN

*Earth with its gnatlike hordes and its whole pitiful routine*

Early evening in Torshavn, Faroe Islands—
music of children shouting in the last light
under a roiled heaven,
the sea rolling and flashing, centuries
of wreckage in its depths.

But always music: whistle and trombone,
string quartet, quartet for three voices and bottle.
Seven Aeolian harps once sang
from the windswept village's church tower,
sorrow aspiring into the stars.

Rollicking tragedy drives the action:
Ura's house on a rock,
her ancient dwelling at last blown from its mooring, tumbles
into the sea, taking her with it
like Icarus—fall of overweening youth
and stubborn, old woman the same.

Learning the woman he loves is also his sister,
Oluf sets ablaze his father's loft,
ending a love story of *intense but pitiful happiness*
which might make you remember your youth.

And still music. As if Orpheus had remained in Hades
with his Eurydice and continued to play
his ascending arias from the inferno.

Heinesen's Orpheus escapes an insular purgatory
with his violin. His uncle Sirius—bright star,
hapless poet, escapes life, his poems at last
streaming after him like the sun's posthumous rays
through torn clouds on the horizon.

Nothing is settled. No grand finale.
Just the music: violin cello bottle whistle:
thin streams like what issued from the ancient water pump
achieving nothing against Oluf's blaze
but an admirable effort nonetheless.

# MERCY

Dunblane, Scotland, 1996


Christmas, the bitter season. The fat red breast
of the chaffinch brightens the hedgerows, sharpens the cold.


With the uneasy residents of North Sea winds
it sings, *None escape the bad beauty.* Sings *Solace.*


I climbed the snow above our Highland hotel
to the top of the mountain alone, my marriage just ended,


hoping to triumph. My son and daughter were off on their own.
No triumph after all, but relief to hear them, as I stumbled
        back down,


so afraid of more loss, their voices at first faint. How
my breath caught to see them emerge over the ridge behind me,


Paul's wild hair, tall Emily in her sky-blue jacket, my two,
my grown children, companions on my escape from the
        ruined holiday.


At our hotel, surrounded by hikers' tents,
sparkling with frost, a sign read *Please do not camp here.*


*Heartrending,* our host said of the deer,
down from the hills, under their saddles of ice.

He fed them kitchen scraps in the hotel parking lot.
He'd named them: *Marianne, Miss Sophisticate,* and *Nestor.*

*They come at sunrise and sunset,* he said,
*When the sky glows on the horizon like a burner.*

Sunset at three in the afternoon, nights adamantine
in their black silence. Hoping for comfort,

I led us Christmas Day to Dunblane Cathedral.
We took our seats amid scraping chairs as the children fidgeted.

Someone moved so we could sit together.
Someone showed us the place in the hymnal.

We didn't remember the massacre of the school children,
until, startled by tears when the choir sang

"Away in a Manger," we realized we were in the sanctuary
with the parents of the remaining children.

The tall, black-robed priest prayed *for those*
*whose pain and isolation deepen in the festive season.*

*Let streams roiling under ice,* he prayed, *map sunlight*
*seeking a home on the wary earth.*

*Let the deer come trusting to be fed,*
*the wanderer find a hearth to shelter him.*

*What is the gift,* he said, *but the Birth*
*in a night of chaos, for the worried, hope,*

*for the lonely, love, for the frightened, courage.*

We sang hymns in the Cathedral
with the bereaved, the remaining children now grown

and reaching across the world to us in sympathy
for our fear that does not abate.

We cannot trust. Forgive us

come spring and summer, come the Birth
again.

# THE BARE TREES

It's not summer's greenery I love but winter's
deciduous branches yearning upward, sky falling into them,
blue or darker blue, a star or two descending slowly, limb to limb.

Like an argument they proceed, more often than not
complex but every iteration visible, one growing directly from the other.

Last summer in a storm, the robin's nest blew to the ground.
We hadn't even known about it, it was so hidden, the eggs now broken.

So many false promises in this world. Accept one,
and your life can be ruined forever.

New Year's Eve, along the avenue, alders reached into the early
        evening sky,
clear and faintly rose-colored. Reached above the traffic,
the walkers, the lit shops, into the no-nonsense emptiness

where beauty offers no meaning, breaks no vows.

# STRANGE MUSIC

The horses surged alongside the fjord,
up past the guesthouse, into the meadow
where a farmer flung hay from his tractor.

Their manes flew
    like the windblown meadow's grass.

I watched as they followed him,
resolving into single file. Then I lost them.

Midnight in the north—

One or two whimbrels called all the dusky night,
    back and forth, near and far.

I could say the agitation in the birches was sky
    haunting all that sang there, homesick
        for what sang there.

The horses came back next morning
singly and in twos and threes
outside my window, bending their necks to the earth

as if in another life I'd called them back
and they'd remembered.

# IN ICELAND WITH PAUL

He got us out of Reykjavik
in spite of the directions. Onto the Ring Road,
almost empty, while I hung out the window
photographing rocky troll faces,
columns offshore, the sentinels
of Dyrgikaet-Reynisdrangar looming,

black-robed judges rising
out of the blue sea into the blue sky.
So much to see—
heroically, he kept his eyes on the road
except for the marvels
we had to stop for.

We ran out of clean clothes—
no usable laundry anywhere,
bought tee shirts at the one-stop stores
along the way—where
you could buy Icelandic sweaters,
skir, and lamb hotdogs.

My driver, my companion
on this risky experiment, mother
and newly divorced son, we traveled
alone together. We rode horses—
one ran away with him—and, his choice,
snowmobiles on the glacier.

My choice—a puffin-watching "hayride,"
a rattley open wagon
behind a tractor, rain slapping
like wet sheets, over black sand
and silver sun streaks.
We arrived at a mountainous dune

and climbed, he easily,
me struggling behind him,
to the top where the puffins nested,
a flat landscape covered
with lush moss ledges sheltering families
with their enormous orange beaks.

Afterward, my camera soaked,
faces and hands blue with cold,
we descended,
back to the wagon,
another brain jangling ride
through the rain to our car.

He played loud music
the whole trip. I loved how
a single bird might call through
an enormous silence.
He loved the strenuous hiking.
I braced myself on his shoulders heading down.

At our last stop, he went off in the long sunset
to find a tavern, a meeting place,
and found nothing. I watched him return,
his characteristic tilt,
walking briskly, a man, alongside the fjord,
the incandescent cliffs.

I felt the old joy
I used to feel
when he slammed the door every evening
at suppertime, *Mom, I'm home!*
dropping his basketball
loudly on the floor.

# SLEEPING WITH ANIMALS

Bugsy, the dachshund,
Celia, my aging mutt, and Fredthecat
sleep on my bed, snoring gently, occasionally farting.

No other sounds. The birds that during the day scatter seeds
all over my porch, the squirrel that swings on the feeder,
sleep nearby in their hiding places.

My son used to sleep crowded
by the German Shepherd sprawled on his small bed.

It is said the Child slept, warmed in the breath of cattle and sheep.

Out the window, the bare alder veins the sky,
offers no protection. Sirius, bright as a strobe,
follows his Orion down, branch to branch, hour by hour.

I am beyond a star's lyrical promise.
Promise does not interest me. Animals live in the present

where we huddle together, dumb and safe.

## JANUARY 19, 2017

The stick bounces on the lake
frozen where the sun has not touched it;
A single crow lands on a branch lying motionless
on the surface, jumps to the ice
and strolls toward shore.
Out in the open, water shines like chrome.
The gold of autumn—yellow leaves raining
through the bluish air, a forest upside down
along the shore—has drifted
to another part of the world.
Runners are running,
dogs walking and loping, crows racketing
in the treetops. Hundreds of widgeons
mill about on the ground.
The dachshund digs in the mulch,
trotting from smell to smell. Once in a while,
he rushes the ducks, and each time,
the witless crowd rises and squawks.
I could be happy today.

# WINTER SCENE IN MOONLIGHT, 1869

Henry Farrer, The Metropolitan

Copses of trees threading the air
like vascular systems dwarf the small evergreens.

Tattered clouds streak the sky, but none
cover the flat moon's worried face.
No human or animal enlivens the scene.
Stars drift around the moon
in a sky the color of bluebirds.

It was a landscape like this where we—
husband, three children and I—
drove across the mountains to see Kahoutec,
the comet allegedly visible before dawn.

I don't remember much, a white expanse
dotted with grasses like this one,
the five of us crowded in the car.
We missed it, gave up and piled
into a motel room to sleep, the family we were.

In those years, my small son delivered newspapers
before sunrise. One January, it snowed for a week,
the snow too deep for him to pull the sled alone.
Every morning, his sister and I went with him
through the pillowy predawn light.
I never liked sending him out in the dark.
How do we bear loving a child?

One night, his father dying,
this child called me away from the sickbed,
called me outside to see
the ring around the moon. We stood together,
my arm around his shoulder, his around my waist,
stood a long time, momentarily happy
under the warm, ruddy wheel, the moon
a friendly eye that shone on us.

I keep coming back to it—
an empty field and the cracked
frozen stream beside the one tree
missing half its branches, casting a crooked shadow.
I'm drawn by an emptiness I understand now—

shadows revealing the light falling over a field

where what has been lost wanders unseen

but palpable, in what the artist has so carefully

rendered in each of the stripped trees—

their intricate, detailed supplications transparent,

drawing the eye to all they do not hide.

# DEPOT BAY, OREGON, ECLIPSE

In the Travelodge parking lot, a few people
have their eclipse glasses on already.
The fog has thinned just in time.

I cross the street to the ocean side
where a small crowd has gathered around a kiosk
offering information, coffee and souvenirs.
I do not buy an eclipse sweatshirt.

We watch the sun slowly shrink to a sliver.
Then, that celestial sunflower,
that stern black angel haloed in white fire
solitary in the empty sky. How little we matter in the end.

A man next to me, elderly, from Kentucky,
says, *I can't see anything.*

*Take your eclipse glasses off, Frank,* his wife says.

*Oh!* He marvels. *Look at that circle. Look, there's a star.*

# NOCTURNE

Shall I write about spiders? Not the big hairy ones,
though I have nothing against them, but the tiny orb weavers
whose miraculous constructions zing between branches.
One billows midway between the wind chimes and the roof.

Across the street, my neighbor practices the piano.
He is timid, his playing careful.

More bad news today about the fires in California.
Iceland's melting, the world's structures faltering.

But tonight, I could believe the few stars visible in the faded city sky
are friendly, sending tentative strobes
through the dogwood leaves, the broken strains of Chopin.

Have I retreated into minutiae,
into the measurable and safely inconsequential?

Spiders weave and reweave their webs
around the porch light, and George's music floats
through the night air like rain in a dry season.
He would probably stop if he knew I were listening.

# AFTERLIFE

Botswana, Okavango Delta


Jacanas stepped leaf to leaf. Hippos dozed,
barely visible in glare.

*If you fall out,* our guide said,
*They will kill you.* Two women, marriages capsized,

we'd blown our savings on this trip.
We'd do anything, thrilled

by the sudden appearance of a crocodile
like a log against the bank, size of two canoes, thrilled

by the malachite kingfishers tipping one reed after another,
close enough to touch, to draw our gaze

from the dangerous magnificent
to the minuscule—red beak and breast, white collar

under its bluer than heaven cloak.
The low sunlight streamed into the river, sky and water

burning behind backlit palms and rain trees,
a slow descent from fire to darker fire,

embers still glowing after we landed, still lighting
a silhouetted man in a mokoro poling along the bank

while a hippo's *Whump whump* called us out
into our broken-open world.

# THIRST

Zebra, Gemsbok, desert elephants, buffalo
come to the waterhole on the desert floor—
stark blue beneath the lodge from where I watch—
a procession, two by two, in threes and fours, in small herds.

From plain and thicket they come to drink, leave,
and then the next arrive, peaceful, back and forth—
to shore, away from shore—

then return to the desert, unforgiving, ferocious clarity
of land and sky—thirst slaked.

The blue of that sky rains all day into the thirst it cannot slake.

A lion roars.

Back home, my children grown, each navigates
a new wilderness.
The more I love, the more my life is fragile.

Ask me what it means to be human.

Imagine an infant's miniature, perfect hands,
its terrifying fontanel.

Imagine what it means to thirst,
to find a watering place, drink deep

then hear the desert calling you back.

# LA NATURA MORTE

Pitti Palace, Florence, 1998

Faithless color—fall's
brash yellows and burgundies,
the weathered barn abandoned

by red. Gray overtakes
a peach's sunny skin,
youth's burnished hair.

These artists know beauty's
mortal, how blind we are
to decay's inelegant finale.

Flowers fountain from vases and jars.
Underneath any of them,
a few already drooping,

you might see a moth,
a small serpent, a gargoyle
camouflaged in leaves

drying around a failed bud.
A skull tilts on a surface
heaped with mussels and clams.

In this one—an apple placed
next to a knife—what's this
an alabaster hand?

Just a hand, slender,
pink nails, a white hand, not
hacked from an arm

but lying palm up,
ready to receive the perfect
red apple

before its color flees,
before scarlet chooses
its darker vocation.

# THIS OCTOBER

Outside the coffee shop, dusk quickens, a welcome chill
against my face.
The old air raid tower looms next to the tiny park where no one stops

between the neighborhood center and the piano store.
Destruction fills the news kiosks on this corner

where an air raid, at least, seems quaint.
Inside the shop, the same crowd studies the bulletin board:

handwritten ads for massage, a Presence workshop, a Tai Chi class,
a dog walker, a guitar, an accountant for Creative People.

Mothers arrange enormous strollers around the small tables,
talking urgently, the babies babbling and gnawing snacks.

Dare I say impermanence casts a permanent light
on this neighborhood where I have lived for years

so far? Dare I say I am happy in this rosy dusk billowing briefly
yet again into the street just as the lights blink on?

Later, I will hear the visiting candidate.
Will I remember everything she says? Probably not

in this blessed chaos blowing all of us moored
each to her own fate. I was once startled to see the sun

shining a single ray on a Steller's jay sailing, blue wings
under the arc of a double rainbow. I took it as a sign.

Of what, I never decided. This flurry of evening
happens again and again as if for the first time, a kind of order

after all. Summer has finally gone. Good riddance I say.
Good riddance to daylight clinging past its welcome.

The artist lies on a pavement
as rain falls on him, gets up and photographs his shape

before it vanishes. A young couple laughs,
chasing a broken umbrella lurching up the street.

# REREADING CAMUS'S *THE PLAGUE*

My favorite moment—when Rieux and Tarrou leave Oran
and the pestilence for a brief swim in the sea. Sitting on the rocks,
they gaze at the quiet waves, *supple and sleek as a creature of the wild,*
surprised to share a moment of happiness that forgets nothing.

They undress and dive in, swimming together under the moon
and stars turning reliably through a universe indifferent
to the suffering that exhausts them every day. Two explorers
tethered only one to the other, they swim with matching strokes

cleansed, we'd like to think, in the night's currents.
They will return to the monotony of their labor
under the icy heaven. One of the last to fall ill,
Tarrou will die. They have embraced without belief or question

the life that has fallen to them, risked that life day in, day out
toiling in the hopeless fields. The plague will die down.
There will be dancing in the streets and fireworks,
the town returned to its somnolent days and heedless nights.

Rieux, his wife dead in a distant city, knows such joy is always
imperiled, that the plague lies dormant over years—
will find us, as it has today, when we were looking somewhere else.
Without belief, I look, late at night

into the sky where Orion pauses, mid stride,

in the silk tree's limbs, Sirius, distance unchanging behind.

# TIDE

Glosa

*The blue sky's engine drone is loud.*
*We're on the scene of a worksite that's trembling.*
*Where ocean depths can suddesnly be revealed—*
*Shells and telephones whispering.*

> Thomas Tranströmer, "Under Pressure,"
> trans. Patty Crane

It's a work in progress, the ocean surface
battling itself and flailing at the continents,
waves radiating like a giant gong.
Is it like the gravity pulling grief forward
until it dissipates on a beach scattered
with little shells and sand dollars?
Hard to hear the sky in such a commotion.
But when an airbus lumbers, at first silent,
a slow-gliding silver wasp,
the blue sky's engine drone is loud.

A work in progress, of course, the world
we know, blue morning-glory taking over
the hopeless shed, hiding or redeeming,
who can say? But crumbling neighborhoods,
cities on fire—destruction will be followed
by the new, we choose to say—the razed house
rebuilt with elegant, grained timbers, ruddy in late sun
where husband and wife finally admit,
after years of lying to themselves, love's dead.
We're at the scene of a worksite that's trembling.

But there's no end to the possible:
revelation may be at hand, new love, a windfall,
the war will end. The dead will stop
calling and complaining to the living
who will someday stop mourning. A child can go
down the street to buy bread. The child will come back.
The graves will be found, one by one,
the camps emptied, homes found for all the dispossessed,
but only after we've fallen deep enough
where ocean depths can be suddenly revealed.

The possible. A jar found on a beach

where I was happy, and the sky grew larger

and bluer all day long until late, when pelicans

rowed over the sea. I saw families,

children and dogs, silhouettes in a windy ballet

with kites, gulls and swinging tides,

sun shafts ripping through storm clouds on the horizon.

There you've been, loves of my life.

There you've changed me, one by one,

all of you, in the one place, bizarre music rioting,

shells and telephones whispering.

# ACKNOWLEDGEMENTS

Thanks to the following print and online journals
where these poems first appeared.

*ONE:*
"Thirst," "Mercy," "Orfeo," "This October."

*SHARK REEF:*
"The Bare Trees," "Festival,"
"Deathbed Drawing of Keats by Joseph Severn."

*ALASKA QUARTERLY REVIEW:*
"Afterlife."

*FLOATING BRIDGE REVIEW:*
"Mockingbird," "Sleeping With Animals."

*NELLE:*
"Purple," "Nocturne."

*CROSSWINDS POETRY JOURNAL:*
"October," "Emily's Tomatoes."

*PRAIRIE SCHOONER:*
"Tide."

*CONNECTICUT RIVER REVIEW:*
"Rereading Camus's *The Plague*."

SPECIAL THANKS to Lise Goett, who gave final shape to this book, whose vision and expertise made it more than the sum of its parts.

Thanks also to John Marshall and Christine Deavel, for casting their gimlet eyes on the early manuscript and offering innumerable helpful edits. Heartfelt thanks also for their steadfast friendship and support through trying times.

Thanks to Melinda Mueller for travels together and long friendship through some of the hardest times of my life.

Thanks also to poet friends Alicia Hokanson, Sherry Rind, Mercedes Lawry, Susan Lane, Judith Skillman, Joannie Stangeland and Lillo Way, whose ongoing support and attention make the writing possible.

And of course, thanks to Lauren Grosskopf, who has made this whole process a pleasure.

I credit my late mother, who played the violin and practiced every morning early, with making music so much a part of my life that I took it for granted.

And always, love and gratitude to Emily Pitkin and Paul Pitkin, my stalwarts.

# NOTES

In Section 1 of *But Still, Music,* I refer to what happens across the fence from my house. In the segregated South, where I grew up, the "colored" poor lived across the fence that separated my yard from Shantytown. This was not unusual, though the caste system was rigid. Most middleclass families employed black maids (at low wages) to clean their houses and take care of their children as intimate parts of the household.

Episodes in "Reading William Heinesen" are taken from a series of stories in *Laterna Magica,* translated by Tiina Nunnaly. The epigraph is from the same source.

"Mercy" – In 1996, The Dunblane massacre took place at Dunblane Primary School in Scotland on March 13. Thomas Hamilton shot dead sixteen pupils and one teacher. He injured 15 others before killing himself. We went to Christmas services in Dunblane Cathedral that year, with the families who lost children in that massacre.

Epigraphs are taken from:
Tomas Tranströmer – *The Sad Gondola,* trans Robin Fulton (1996)
Hjaldor Laxness – *World Light,* trans Magnus Magnussen (1969)

The boy in the photograph is Michael.

ANNE PITKIN grew up in the South, Clarksville, TN, when it was still a small town. She attended Vanderbilt University when the Civil Rights Movement was getting underway. She graduated just after Bloody Sunday, the march across the Edmund Pettus Bridge. Some of the poems in this collection are about growing up as a privileged white child in the segregated South.

Anne moved to Bellingham, WA when she married and subsequently to Seattle, where she has lived ever since.

She has two grown children and two grandchildren. Their mother, her eldest, died three years ago. Many of the poems here address that loss.

Anne is a retired community college English instructor. She went back to school and became a psychotherapist, sometimes practicing while still teaching. She is retired from both now. She plays jazz piano with her friends, pandemic permitting. She currently lives with her two dogs, Riley, an oversized Pomeranian and Klaus, a mini dachshund.

This is her third full length collection, preceded by YELLOW and WINTER ARGUMENTS, and a chapbook NOTES FOR CONTINUING THE PERFORMANCE. Her poems have appeared in *Poetry Chicago, Prairie Schooner, Alaska Quarterly Review, One, New Orleans Review, New England Review, Rattle* and many others.

CPSIA information can be obtained
at www.ICGtesting.com
Printed in the USA
JSHW021505190822
29483JS00003B/142